How Not to Be A Prat

By Ali Newport

Published by New Generation Publishing in 2020

First Edition

ISBN: 978-1-78955-881-4

www.newgeneration-publishing.com

New Generation Publishing

I dedicate this book to my parents, Sue and Don; my partner Stacey; the memory of my Granddad Dennis; and my son Woody.

Woody is currently still incubating in my partner's uterus. My challenge is to finish this book before he pops his little head out, and is definitely my biggest motivation for writing this. Thank you Little Man!

INTRODUCTION

Let me set the scene for you….

It is the 18th August 2019. I am sitting in seat '29D' on an Iberia Airlines flight from Madrid to London Gatwick. In row twenty-eight, just in front of me sits my partner Stacey, twenty-three weeks pregnant with our son, Woody.

Now you might make the assumption that Stacey and I are budget flyers and have declined to pay the extra money to choose our exact seats so we could sit together; and whilst I do like to get a deal where I can and try and budget where necessary; sadly that is not the case with this flight…..

Sitting over three economy plane seats with your legs up and stretching out sounds like a really comfortable way to fly, but when your right leg is in a temporary plaster cast following a broken fibula bone at the point where it connects to your ankle, I can assure you from experience that it is really, really not!

During this not so luxurious flight, I had plenty of time to do a little thinking.

My head went closer to the gap between the seats in front and I said to Stacey, "I could have anywhere from six to twelve weeks of being glued to a sofa, not being able to walk and getting bored out of my skull. I'm going to write a book about something."

To which she replied, "What's the book gonna be about, and what are you gonna call it?"

"No idea" I said.

To which she replied one of the funniest yet possibly most helpful things I've ever heard her say… "How about, How Not to Be A D**K?!"

As you read further on, you will understand exactly what she meant and why something along these lines was such a suitable title for this book!

It was at this exact point in time (I am going to make a fairly educated guess now that I am not the only person to have had this thought!) I decided to sit down and sort my life out.

"That's a bit extreme" I hear you mutter, just because of a broken leg, however you have not found out yet how this painful feat was achieved…. We will get to that later on!

Before we go any further, I would just like to make a declaration about the content within this book.

All Events were real events (myself, most people that know me and anyone else involved can promise you that!) and they are all as I remember them. There will be a few bits of detail that will be left out here and there and this is purely because some things were a long time ago and I don't have the best memory in the world!

The intention of this book is not to tell anyone what he or she should or shouldn't do. I had huge problems with this when I was growing up and I am sure that my parents and School and College teachers can confirm this, so I am not about to try and do the same.

Sharing my experiences with you is hopefully just a light read for your enjoyment, and as I try and explain what I have or haven't learnt, it is entirely up to you what you choose to do with the information!

1. THIS IS ME

Do not worry.... Whether you are or are not a fan of 'The Greatest Showman' this chapter has absolutely nothing to do with the song content of the afore mentioned film (phew!).

After having a conversation with my sister, Emily (who now resides in Australia) and discussing this book with her it was agreed like most things that it is best to start from the beginning:

I was born to my parents on the 13th January 1985. By the end of this book you might think it fitting that it was to be Friday 13th, but sorry to disappoint, it was actually a Sunday!

From stories my parents tell me, my siblings tell me and what I remember, you could say I was pretty much a prat from the day I was born!

Now I am not trying to make excuses and defend anything I have done in my past, but I would just like to introduce you to the concept of 'Second Child Syndrome'.

Second or Middle Child Syndrome is a feeling of exclusion by a middle child. This effect occurs because the first child is more prone to receiving privileges and responsibilities being the oldest, while the youngest in the family is more likely to receive indulgences. The second or middle child no longer has their status as the baby and seems to be left with no clear role in the family, or a feeling of being left out.

So, Yep! You guessed it.... This is me!

I had an older sister and in time two younger brothers so my behaviour and the way I acted growing up was probably not helped by my position in the family.

Up until the age of twenty-three, when I moved out of home and spread my wings, I grew up with my family on a 'smallholding' or 'hobby farm'. We have always had fields and land, so I managed to spend a lot of my youth hanging out with friends who had adjoining properties, driving cars and motorbikes off road at the age of thirteen, shooting rabbits, drinking and smoking lots of pot (weed, cannabis, marijuana, resin, skunk…. lots to list and pretty much had them all at some point). From my own personal experience, I loved this part of my childhood!

If I asked my parents about stories of me and what I was like growing up, I am sure this book would end up being the first of a trilogy set!

Due to the experiences I later put my parents through, which you will read in this book, I decided I didn't really need to open up old wounds again so thought I would only share a few things with you that I remember….

Keeping horses was always a keen interest of my parents so inevitably, I was what I like to call, 'born into it'. I was riding at a young age on the ponies we would keep and one thing I would just like to say here is my Mum always said I was 'a natural' and could do well if I applied myself properly!

I think this phrase could well have been true in many other aspects of my life, but I think I always seemed to struggle with the part that says: "Applied myself properly!!!".

Around the age of eight we had a white pony I used to frequently ride called 'Magic'. What wasn't so magic was the time I decided the best way to transport a bucket from one end of the outdoor arena to the other whilst riding the horse was over my riding hat, on my head.

Of course, I couldn't see a single thing and one thing leads to another and before you know it, I'm lying flat out on the floor having been chucked off!

4

After removing the bucket so I could eventually see, there was my Mum, my sister and even Magic all thinking "What a prat!".

This was definitely a sign of things to come and was a sort of induction into the new realms of being a complete twat at times.

As I got older and grew bigger, I chopped in the ponies and upgraded to the bigger horses, but with no more common sense than I had at the age of eight with a bucket on my head.

As you can imagine, the final showdown did not end well....

I think I was about fourteen the last time I rode a horse. I was out on a hack with my sister Emily, riding a lovely horse we had at home called Jasper. He was a fairly large palomino and had a very good nature.

Emily and I weren't far from home when we decided to have a bit of a canter down the straight track we were on. Now, if you know me well, you'd know that I love a bit of speed! I wouldn't call myself an adrenaline junkie, but I have bungee jumped, skydived, participated in off-road rallying, own and ride a 990cc motorbike and many other things that just give me a buzz!

On this particular day I was in front of Emily and was enjoying the canter, but it just wasn't enough. I stepped Jasper up a gear and now we were galloping down the track.

I was enjoying this immensely till I realised that the trees and foliage either side of the track were starting to become slightly blurred. I can only assume that Jasper was enjoying the speed as much as I was, but then the thought crossed my mind asking, "Is this a bit too fast?!".

The smile I had on my face had started to straighten out and now it was turning upside down. Emily was on an older, smaller, slower horse, and was left way behind so I knew it was just me and Jasper.

Now if you ride or have ever ridden a motorbike, scooter or even a pushbike, then I am sure you will be able to relate very well to this bit…. If you haven't then I am sure you will still get the gist where I am coming from.

Riding a horse has a similar sensation to riding a bike. You are sitting astride a 'vehicle' and with either the reigns in hand, or handlebars in hand, you like to think you are in control of what the chosen vehicle will do.

If you go too fast then you release the throttle, apply the brakes if need be or you sit back in the saddle and pull on the reigns slightly saying 'whoa' or something similar and you reach the desired speed.

In this instance what I thought would work, didn't and I now realised I had absolutely no control whatsoever. With the adrenaline rushing through my veins and a lot of my energy being used up to hold my bum cheeks together, I glanced ahead of me and saw something I didn't like the look of. It was a hefty wooden gate spanning the whole of the track and very much shut!

I used all the remainder of my energy to pull on the reigns as hard as I could and leaned back in the saddle to try and stop, but to no avail. The gate rushed towards me and within seconds I heard an almighty crash, I was flung up in the air and came to rest in a heap on the ground.

By the time Emily caught up, I was still lying on the ground, a little bit dazed with an even more confused Jasper standing over me probably trying to understand why I hadn't opened the gate.

Luckily, there were no life-threatening injuries to be had on this occasion. When I was pulling so hard on the reigns, I had pulled Jaspers head to the side, and as I was hanging on for dear life, he physically couldn't see the direction he was running in. This destroyed the idea I had that just maybe he would jump the gate when we got there.

My sister rode home to alert my Mum to what had happened and they then drove down the track and loaded me into the car to take me back. I managed to sustain some pretty bad bruising on my legs where they had acted as a buffer between Jasper's chest and the gate as he forced it open with all the horsepower he could muster! Other than that, pride was the only other thing damaged!

Following this drama, I decided to transfer any more riding of horses to the riding of motorbikes. I feel I am in full control of a motorbike, if it throws me off it would more than likely be my fault and unlike a bloody horse a motorbike doesn't have the capacity to think for itself!

With these misdemeanours with the horses, pulling my sisters shorts down (whenever it was embarrassing and inappropriate to do so with the present company), calling my brothers names until they couldn't stop crying, and other things I am not proud of, I think I managed to push my parents to the limit on many occasions.

I have no doubt that my difficult behaviour contributed to the need for an Au-pair during my childhood, and we grew up with a number of them visiting from different countries such as Sweden, Germany, France, Holland and others. Some would stay for 6 months, others for a year, and of course there were one or two that didn't last long at all!

I think I got along with them all pretty well…. That was up until we had a Hungarian male whom I did not particularly like!

The straw that I think broke the camel's back was when I had taken the piss out of him constantly about his use of English and words he mispronounced during lunch. My cousins were with me and if I have an audience, then I do try and put on a show!

The only reason I stopped winding him up on this particular

7

day was because I was running out of the kitchen top speed towards the stairs. He had obviously had enough and as he jumped up from his seat, I thought he was going to attack me with the breadboard, Red Leicester cheese or whatever he could pick up first.

This was flight or fight and I was straight for the flying option. So much so that I headed up the stairs, across the landing and straight through a small window out on to a flat roof of the house. Luckily, he decided not to pursue me any further as I had run out of options of where to go, however he locked the window behind me and waited for my Mum to get home.

She fought my corner when she returned home and from memory, I don't think we had him living with us for much longer!

***

Looking back now and after numerous discussions I have had with my Mum in the past I fully appreciate that I was an awkward child for her to single handily raise while my Dad worked long hours in the city as the bread winner of the family.

The 'Second Child Syndrome' I mentioned earlier, I think could have been a small factor in why I was the way I was but I'm not using this as an excuse. I think it was just attention from my Mum that I very much wanted. In my world, even negative attention is attention.

Once I had made it through Junior School, my Secondary School and then College years hold very fond memories for me, whether for the right reasons or not! I managed to start growing up somewhat, maturing and finding my real self through this time.

I wasn't the most academic of people and I definitely wasn't exactly following in my older sisters' footsteps. She was a 'straight A' sort of student and I was more of a 'straight, I'll

8

do whatever the heck I feel like doing today' sort of student. She was a hard act to follow.

I did manage to achieve certain things however:

I achieved obtaining numerous detentions for varying reasons, being put on report in school twice and college once, suspended from college for two weeks, lack of attendance for most lessons most weeks and a few other things! I was lucky enough to leave school and college with pretty reasonable grades despite the very large lack of effort I put in and if I had 'applied myself properly' (as my Mum used to say!) probably would have been a very different story.

Would I have enjoyed it as much though?

I think I can confidently say: "No, I wouldn't have!".

I had worked out by this stage of my life, I wasn't cut out to be an academic, I was an entertainer!!

Sometimes a bit of a prat but entertaining none the less!

I formed a strong group of close friends at this time, and am lucky enough that we still get together a couple of times a year at least to catch up. As well as these guys, I wanted to be everyone's friend and if I could do something to gain attention then I would find a way!

Here is a perfect example:

'MOT' stands for 'Men On Top'. Four of my good friends and I formed a boy band for a talent show in our last year at Secondary School. We put so much effort into what we were doing and loved every minute of it. The band got back together in the second year of College and also performed at a small intimate gig for a friend's birthday.

Don't know whether you have guessed right or not but of course we were bloody awful! We did covers of 'Westlife' and 'Boyzone', pretty much couldn't hold a single note, timing was all over the place, but the main thing was we had a right laugh doing it and gave great amusement to everyone that had to endure a performance.

For me, this is a great example to show that you can sometimes be a bit of a prat, but with purely positive consequences. Maybe it is not that often, but it is definitely possible…. Just like the cop's, there is a 'Good Prat: Bad Prat'!

2. SUDDEN CHANGE IN MY LIFE

Have you ever said to yourself or any of your mates after a night out: "Seemed like a great idea at the time!"??

The majority of silly stories by most people can usually be associated with this comment.

This, however on the rarer occasions is not always the case...

The date is 3rd October 2003. I am eighteen years old, recently left College and currently earning a wage working as a waiter and barman in a local village pub. At this age I had a pretty carefree attitude about most things in life. I wasn't really sure what I wanted to do as a career and with the enjoyment of still living at home, paying minimal rent and being looked after very well by my parents when I needed something, I felt that right now life was good.

As I had turned eighteen at the beginning of this year and could now actually legally drink, going out and having a laugh would happen most Thursday, Friday and Saturday evenings and some weeks it would happen every night, as there was nothing stopping me not to do so.

However, the incident that happened this night, I can confidently say, changed my life forever.

3rd October this year was a Saturday. From memory it was a fairly mild evening and booked in the diary was a good friend's mother's wedding reception that I was attending with him and his girlfriend. This celebration was being held in a popular pub in town probably not more than five miles from my parent's house where I lived.

The dress code for this night out was smart/casual, so I felt it was time to wear my favourite clothing for a good time.... This consisted of my Levi 501 Jeans; a blue, white and red stripy shirt; and my 'lady killer' shoes as I used to call them. These were a pair of pure snakeskin beauties!

The evening rolled on nicely and other than meeting a few people I already knew and meeting some new people I didn't, it was an enjoyable fault free evening; up until the time we left.

My friend, who's mother's celebration it was had decided to be driver for the evening. As this was a night of celebration and no driving for me, I managed to assume the role of chief drinker and was satisfied with how I performed this, once the time came to leave the venue.

I have learnt that all actions have consequences and if you can see that before you carry out the actions, you are much better prepared to make the decision whether to proceed with what you are going to do or not.

Do you remember when you are growing up and your parents put you in your car seat and they strap you in. Then you grow out of the child seat and upgrade to the booster seat. Then you start learning to drive, learning the Highway Code and one of the first and I will agree most important rules is… WEAR A BLOODY SEATBELT.

Upon leaving, I slumped into the back of the three-door hatchback, put no seat belt on and decided it was comfier to lay across all three of the back seats. This was possibly one of the worst ideas I have ever had and links straight to - "Seemed like a good idea at the time" and "How not to be a prat!"

There was a nice quiet road that acted as a great short cut from where the venue was, to where my parents lived, and as you near the main road there is a small chicane with the first corner at the bottom of a small hill and the second corner slap bang right at the top of a second hill.

The problem that these small cars have negotiating this sort of road layout is that there is a limit of the speed at which you can enter them. If you just push your speed even between 5-10mph too much, then what happens is the car hits the first corner at the bottom of the hill quite hard. At this point, you have just about got around the first corner but now find that because of the speed you hit the incline, the front suspension has bounced the front wheels of your car off the road marginally. Trying to travel up a hill at speed, approaching a tight corner and then realising your car doesn't seem to be steering at all is more than just a little worrying!

By now you have your front wheels on full lock to steer around the corner you are virtually going around but find that traction is still an issue as the wheels have still not got full contact with the road yet.

The next part all happened fairly quickly for me.

The cars wheels finally touched down on the tarmac in a full lock position with the anticipation it would eventually make it around the corner. It didn't. The speed the car was still travelling and the position of the wheels, instantly threw the vehicle over sideways onto its roof and into a spin with myself and the other two passengers feeling like we were on a demon of a rollercoaster.

A poorly situated large tree trunk decided this ride was at an end and abruptly ceased the momentum that we had. However the ride wasn't over for me as the sudden impact of the rear of the car (still travelling upside down on its roof) hitting the tree trunk, displaced me from my current lying position, and put me straight through the glass of the rear window where I continued till I met a tree on the side of the road with my head. I finished the ride lying in a field next to the road somewhat battered and bruised.

After eventually being found in the field covered in blood due to the grazing and cuts I sustained going through the rear screen, and accompanied by police and paramedics, I boarded an air ambulance to the nearest local hospital that could carry out emergency procedures straight away due to the risk of a serious head injury being likely.

First hospital was Princess Royal in Haywards Heath; 'no room at the inn'; so I was transferred into an ambulance and taken to King's College Hospital in London. Here I was assessed, and they found that I had sustained a subdural haematoma also known as a brain haemorrhage.

A subdural haematoma is where blood collects between the skull and the surface of the brain. The bleeding and increased pressure on the brain can often be life threatening and it requires operating on as soon as possible to minimise critical damage to the brain.

A 'craniotomy' operation consists of a small disc of skull (also known as a bone flap) being removed to gain access to the brain. Once this is achieved then the trapped fluid can be removed, the bone flap can be replaced with three mini plates and the scalp is then closed up with staples.

Luckily for me, my craniotomy was a success!

The whole procedure lasted about four hours and although the haematoma was successfully removed, that is not the end of the story. Being that this was still a serious brain injury, recovery time can vary massively between individuals, and mine was not helped by contracting the superbug MRSA.

Despite this however, I was fortunate that I had a recovery somewhat on the quicker side. Now, let me tell you, this had nothing to do with the fact that my injury was just a minor bump of the head, oh no! I have the scars to prove that literally! My saving grace was my Mum.

My Mum is a qualified Craniosacral Therapist. Craniosacral Therapy is a complimentary therapy where, through gentle non-manipulative touch, it helps your body's own healing mechanisms to balance, restore and heal your body.

I had a treatment from my Mum every single time she was by my bed when I was in hospital and that was pretty much every day after what I had just been through.

If I am being honest, when friends were asking me how I recovered so quickly from the traumatic injury I had sustained, I told them "coz Mum was giving me treatments every day she was at the hospital".

Most of the time I am met with, what I can only call 'blank' faces. It is a hard conversation to try and explain something that even I don't fully understand! But, in life, I'm sure there are many things that a lot of us can't wholly understand but somehow know just work, and this is certainly one of them.

Even though my Mum was physically helping me in the way that she could, I want to mention my Dad here too.

He had to be the support for my Mum during this time and still had to look after everything that kept moving along at home, none of which stopped, just because I had. Dad always managed to keep everything together however hard the situation was and this has always been something I've admired and looked up to in him for.

I owe so much to my parents, to be here today writing this book.

Some of you reading this may be parents, some may not be and some like myself may be expecting to be very soon. I hope you will never have to go through what my parents did.

After talking with my parents, even I can't begin to understand what they went through the night they received the call from the police telling them that their son was being flown by air ambulance to A&E following a serious car accident. Even writing this now I am welling up a bit!

I bet fear was one of the worst things they were feeling that night driving to the hospital I was destined for, waiting to see whether their son would even still be alive by the time they got there.

After the brain haemorrhage was confirmed the worrying for them really couldn't even be put on hold. A craniotomy operation doesn't come without risks and once this has been completed, the chances of short and long-term damage, both physically and mentally are still possible.

Throughout the weeks of my recovery from the accident, I had been exposed to various drugs and chemicals; anaesthetic for the operation, tablets for the risk of epileptic seizures (the part of the brain I damaged is linked to where epilepsy stems from so the risk of now becoming epileptic increased somewhat), tablets for the pain and others. With these circulating round my bloodstream and after having part of my skull cut out and replaced to be able to drain fluid off my brain, I was not in any state to be understanding what my parents were having to deal with and how much they loved me.

Here are a few of the things they had to put up with once I returned home:

- I suffered with serious bouts of anxiety and stress
- I struggled to sleep
- I cried a lot for no reason at random times
- I wet the bed
- I suffered with extreme memory loss day to day, and didn't always know what I was doing

This was a massive turning point in my life to realise how important family really are, and the people that love you most. There was a chance I wouldn't have made it through this episode of my life, but it obviously just wasn't my time.

One very true fact in life is that everyone will come to an end at some point. Just because this is inevitable, does not mean that you shouldn't cherish every moment you have with the people you love, and don't ever spend time dwelling on the past or regrets.

I've started the book with this story first as it was definitely the biggest thing that has ever happened to me in my life.

"Was it the worst?". I'd say: "Definitely not!".

"Why not?" (I hear you ask!).

Well, this is why…...

I feel that sometimes things happen in your life because they are meant to.

Let me first emphasise that this was a horrible experience to go through and something I wouldn't wish on anyone. What it has done however has given me time to reflect on my life as it was happening up to that point, try and change the direction I was going in, become a better person as best as I can be and adjust to changes that have happened due to the injury.

I am a keen believer in things happening for a reason and I think that for me this accident was always meant to happen.

3. TURNING THE CORNER

In the last chapter I mentioned that the car accident had a definite degree of positivity for me, and just wanted to touch upon some of the positive changes that happened in my life as a consequence; taking something positive out of something so bad.

In Chapter one, where I talked about stories of my younger years, I shared that I had been a user of recreational class B drugs.

I attended several outpatient appointments following my release from the hospital and I will always remember the neurologist that I regularly saw, telling me if I had previously been taking drugs, then it was now definitely time to stop.

Here are some of the varying reasons why:

1. Drugs contain stimulants of varying forms. Cocaine especially has been known to burst blood vessels and is a very likely cause of strokes and even haemorrhages for regular users.

2. Studies in the US have shown people between the ages of sixteen and twenty-five are much more likely to develop an addiction to drugs following any TBI (Traumatic Brain Injury). The best thing here to avoid this risk, is just not to take them at all.

3. After a TBI, thinking, remembering and concentrating can be largely affected. In my circumstance this was a side effect I was left with and the use of drugs is well known to make these problems worse.

4. I contracted MRSA when I was in the hospital where the craniotomy operation was carried out. If I was to take drugs and re-haemorrhage or incur an injury due to the taking of drugs where I had the operation and this became infected, death is a very high possibility.

There are many other reasons, but these are probably the bluntest and easiest to understand.

As I had been through so much already and felt that I was lucky at this point to be alive, I was not going to jeopardise this again.

Some friends and people I know told me I was lucky to still be around but can get away with anything because I'm like a cat with nine lives. My reply to this was always quite bluntly, "Yeah, but in case you hadn't noticed, I'm not a bloody cat!"

I haven't taken a single drug other than any prescribed medication for almost sixteen years now. Big positive!

***

Another example of something positive I managed to take from my accident is a story involving a friend that I know very well from the village I live in.

One evening, he was out having a drink and a laugh with his mates and had an unfortunate accident on the way home…. Are you familiar at all with the art of 'bush jumping'?

I'm not sure whether it was just something that I grew up with because it was at its peak at this time, or whether it has been around for centuries, maybe going under a different title?!

Anyway, for anyone that doesn't know, 'bush jumping' is when you throw yourself into a generally soft type bush/hedge (the most common time for this activity is when people are on their way home from a big night out!), sink into it, have a quick rest and then get back on your feet with the bush springing itself back into its original shape with none or very minimal damage.

Sadly, for my friend on the night in question, the wrong bush was chosen as it seemed to be someone had buried a trampoline within the foliage. As he jumped into the bush he recoiled straight back out, hitting his head on the kerb, sustaining a not-so-nice head injury.

At the time it didn't seem that there was any worrying damage, however the next morning, headaches, concussion, balance problems and other ailments associated with a bad head injury started to make an appearance. Although not sustaining any form of brain haemorrhage the trauma caused serious bouts of anxiety, stress and depression. All things that I was very familiar with.

Having been through an ordeal like this, what you want to be able to do is talk to someone who actually understands personally what you are going through; and that is literally what we did. We just talked…

He asked questions and I answered them as best I could. One of the best things I said, was to reassure him, that what he was actually going through was normal, and I had been there too and you still get through it in the end.

I take a lot of satisfaction from helping people in any way I can and will always remember this occasion. I am pleased to say that he did make a full recovery (time for thumbs up emoji here!!).

***

After my full recovery from this accident, I tried to just get back to a life as normal as it could be. I decided to take three months off travelling the world and living life making the most of every day. My friends and I made stops in Hong Kong, Melbourne, Sydney and Perth, New Zealand, Fiji and Thailand.

One of my favourite times was journeying through Australia with one of my best mates in a camper van just taking each day as it comes and enjoying living.

When I got back from my travels, I managed to establish a fairly 'normal' routine; I worked for various radio stations, worked as a tradesman, and started doing TV and film extras work (this seemed to satisfy my need to entertain an audience!).

I started looking at properties available in my local area and eventually after eighteen months, managed to find what I was looking for and was the owner of my first house. It just so happens that my house backs on to a recreation ground, which is next to a main road, which has a footpath on the other side, which is only a ten-minute walk to the bottom of my Mum and Dad's fields! It's good not to stray too far away from Mummy and Daddy!

As I settled into my new lifestyle, I found a great group of new friends at the local pub and am pleased to say that I still frequent 'The Shelley Arms' to this day. A lot of these friends are part of the stories that you will read about later on, and over the years have been a major part of my life for varying reasons.

***

I will always be asking myself this same question for the rest of my life. If I had never had the car accident and never had the injury I sustained, would I be where I am now?

I think I will always answer 'No' to this question.

I don't think I would be half the person I am now and have all the things I have going for me, had this accident not been a part of my life. Once you feel that you have been so close to what could have been the end, it makes you appreciate so much more in your life.

Don't get me wrong… I have been, and still am, making mistakes and I'm no saint. Having a major accident and injury is not a remedy that fixes it all in any way, shape or form, but what I have learnt is that however bad something seems to be, if you look closer, there is always something good to be found within it.

4. RELATIONSHIPS

Have you ever had a relationship or two before you have finally met and settled down with the person you're with now?

Well I have.

At the end of each failed relationship (I am not going to talk too much about them in this book as they are a whole story unto themselves!) I would always be saying, "How do I carry on with the rest of my life? I'll never find anyone like her again." and "Why doesn't anyone love me?".

I have now found the answers to these questions.

The answer to the first is simply; stop being a baby, stop wallowing in self-pity, pull your socks up, get back on the horse and bloody go get 'em cowboy!

The answer to the second is; course they do. Stop being an idiot!

Here is how I managed to come to this conclusion.

All my past relationships have had their ups and they have definitely had their downs. If I just look into them a tiny bit deeper, I suddenly find that at certain points in each relationship there has been at least one event or situation that in some way has benefited either them, myself, or both of us.

Whatever this was and whatever I learnt from them, I have definitely taken this new knowledge to the next relationship being a slightly better person.

I had an ex-partner whom I 'clicked' with straight away and then during the early stages of our relationship realised that we got on so well, even though we were actually very different sorts of people. The idea of 'opposites attract' seemed to be doing its job here!

This ex-partner had a very care-free attitude to most things. She liked to be a 'free spirit' as much as she could, dare I say she was very much like a female Peter Pan, a child that never wanted to grow up and had an immense amount of fun whilst doing so. At this stage in my life, I still loved doing fun things, I still loved travelling, loved my diving, enjoyed socialising but also managed to balance this out with what I like to class as 'being life practical'.

What this means was that I had purchased a house, and had a mortgage, ran my own business, was putting money into a pension fund, and was looking forward to settling down with children and a family sometime in the near future.

Sadly, she had other ideas, and although I am sure this led to the demise of our relationship in the end, there are so many ways that she helped me to become a better person...

Have you ever had an old bike in your garage that you haven't ridden for a while, but you always remember that when you did, you had great fun doing so?

Maybe you moved to a new house, maybe you got a new job with longer hours, maybe you had children, maybe 'life' just got in the way?

Every time you walk past the bike, you say to yourself, "I'll clean that up and take it out for a ride on the weekend". But it still sits in the same place, untouched, and evidently you didn't get around to it.

Then one day, your mate cycles past whilst you happen to be looking at the bike again and says, "Why don't you come out for a quick cycle with me?"

Why not!

You grab your helmet, grab the bike and as you pedal off down the road (with rusty gear linkage, no brakes and a flat rear tyre), it fills you with that feeling of immense enjoyment you remember you used to have.

I feel that getting myself back on that bike was what had happened to me. I used to have this child inside me, full of fun and mischief, that made me the person I am, and at this point in my life, he seemed to be having a very long sleep.

My ex-partner managed to wake him up, get him back out and brought me back to my old self again! And thanks to her, I still find that balance in my life, that part of me that was missing is well and truly back and I am extremely grateful to her for that; for helping me find my inner child.

It can take a while to find these positives, from a lot of things you feel were frankly, just really shit! Trust me, they are there; you just need to have a rummage around sometimes to find them.

I think that these past relationships were destined to fail for a reason. I was meant to meet the ex-partners, we were meant to help each other in certain ways, and once we had accomplished that, it was time to move on.

Eventually your paths come to an end as you are now who you need to be. I feel I am now such a better person than I have ever been, I am in the happiest relationship I have ever had with a beautiful young woman and expecting my first child.

It doesn't get much better than that!

***

One of the biggest learning curves for me came from my seven-year relationship that taught me a hell of a lot about life, and about myself.

I was twenty-three, having a quiet drink at my local pub and met this wonderful woman, who had her eighteen- month old child sat beside her.

We got on very well and it wasn't long after this first meet that we were in a relationship together and I was staying at her house often, settling in with this very unfamiliar feeling of being a father type figure in this new family situation.

Soon after this, I had pretty much moved in with her and her son, and as he grew up, there would be taking him to playschool, taking him to school, dropping him to friends' houses and more and more to do as he got older. I surprised myself with how easy I seemed to fit in to this new regime.

Before all this, I enjoyed single life. I liked going out and partying, I liked not having to answer to anyone and I loved having pretty much no responsibility for anyone or anything.

How my life had changed but I seemed to just take it in my stride!

After moving in, and probably three years into the relationship, I started to notice things. I'm not going to bore you with a long narrative of what I picked up on but the long and short of it was that I noticed she was drinking a lot; too often; and I realised that my partner was an alcoholic.

I was with this partner for seven years, had developed a great bond with her and I loved her very much. I want you to understand that all I am doing is explaining my experience and feelings of this time and in no way am I intending for any of this to come across that I am speaking ill of anyone involved.

Contrary to a lot of people thinking an alcoholic is just someone who loves drinking and can't be bothered to stop. Alcoholism IS an illness. Believe me I have experienced it first-hand.

A simple way to try and explain what I was going through, would be to think of yourself trying to fix a punctured bike tyre without a puncture repair kit? You put the air in the tyre, it fills up back to normal for a bit and then it goes back down, and you are back to square one again. Then you can repeat this process over and over again but in the long run, you will never have the tyre actually fixed.

Our relationship began to take on this trait. The key thing I learnt here is that when dealing with this illness, you need to have the personal desire to want to be helped before you can be helped. Sometimes this desire takes longer than you want before it becomes apparent, and sadly in other cases it just doesn't come at all.

Eventually I think we were both struggling to cope with what was going on. We were as stubborn as each other, so when an argument would start about pretty much anything, neither of us would back down. I think this was one of the main things that eventually started to push us apart.

We eventually decided to go our separate ways for varying reasons. This wasn't so much because our feelings had changed for each other at this point, but more that the relationship was not functional and it would be better all-round if we weren't together anymore. A young child was witnessing all of this drama and there was a lot of it he was understanding but also a lot of it that he didn't. He did not deserve to be in this situation.

We did see one another a few times after we split and we stayed in touch, however, to save complicating what was going on, sadly I decided not to see her son anymore on the occasions that we met.

Eighteen months from the time we broke up, she passed away.

I received the phone call late one evening from her ex (her son's father) and he told me the news.

I didn't know how to take something like this at all. My first thing to do was just freeze and try and take it all in. Then I broke down in tears still trying to actually get my head round what I had just been told. In person, she was now gone; forever.

I have had good memories from this time but also many memories that I would rather not remember. Once again though, I have taken my own time to reflect on this and here is where I still see the good.

I am a very open person and I don't get particularly embarrassed about telling people things I have done or been through. Take this book as a prime example!

What I have noticed with certain people within my friendship circle is sometimes people are not as forthcoming as I am when it comes to personal problems and seeking help for these.

My first thing to say is asking for help can be so scary, but once you have taken this step everything becomes so much easier. I am sure you have heard of the saying: "A problem shared, is a problem halved". This is so, so true.

The seven years I spent in this relationship was my first proper experience of being with someone and settling down. I always thought that this was normal, and the way I learned to behave was standard procedure. However, as I met a new partner, it started to become quite obvious to me that the trauma and stress of the relationship had affected me more than I realised and it was time to do something about it.

I found a local therapist who dealt with a multitude of sins and started to see her on a weekly basis. We soon discovered that the main issues I was dealing with at this time were lack of thinking before acting, getting frustrated when I couldn't fix things, with frustration often turning to anger.

At some of my appointments, I got to spend an hour slagging anyone off I chose to, and you would be surprised how much better you feel after getting a lot of stuff off your chest! Once my therapist had decided I was at a stage where she couldn't do anymore for me, I truly believed I was a better person.

A few years after this and following another failed relationship attempt, I decided to see a different therapist who was a good friend of my Mum's. Here, I would just like to thank her so much for what she did for me. I know it is her job and I paid her for it (nothing is free these days!) but it just felt that she was the right person I needed to be seeing and at the right time.

The biggest thing that surfaced when we were talking at these sessions, was that I don't think I had ever been able to properly grieve and deal with the loss of my first partner. 'Bottling things up' is something I managed to master pretty well at a young age and seemed to continue well into my adult life.

If you don't want to become a tangled up, emotional mess then I would advise against this!

I think that these last therapy sessions that I attended, opened up some old wounds but eventually brought me face to face with things I needed to deal with, so I could eventually move on in my life and begin my future in the right direction.

If you feel any connection to what I have just been talking about, let me tell you, it is never too late. There is always someone, somewhere, who will listen.

The 'Love Train' sightseeing tour!

A bit of fun prior to the bucket incident!

It's amazing how much someone can enjoy wheeling their boyfriend through Madrid airport on a baggage trolley with their broken leg!

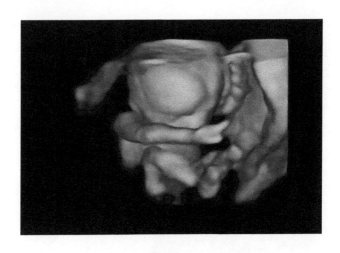

Little baby Woody at 16 weeks

The joys of getting stuck in a table whilst playing the new game, 'Table turtle challenge!'

*Three good friends
enjoying a lovely
Spanish wedding before
one of them does
something stupid...*

*The morning after the
night before with a
broken fibula.*

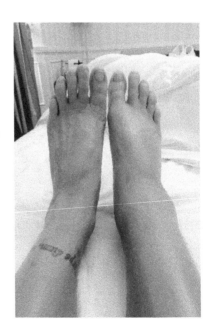

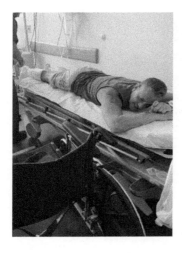

Time for a quick temporary cast to fly home in

The worrying thing is just before surgery, the consultant draws an arrow on your leg, so the surgeons knows which one to operate on!
I thought the boot was a giveaway!!

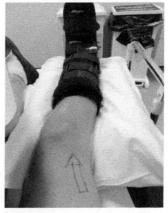

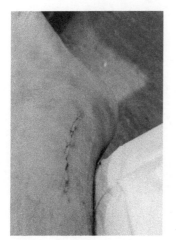

Wound healing nicely after being cut open to have the break plated.

Always need to get yourself in the local paper once in your life (!) and the scars left from the craniotomy operation.

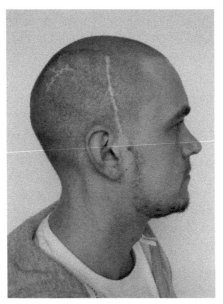

5. THE LOVE TRAIN CALLING AT...

There are three categories that I tend to put people in when it comes to public transport.

The first category is the people that use public transport all the time. They use buses and trains to continually commute to work, maybe don't have a car, or perhaps they just enjoy the unpredictability of these particular modes of transport!

The second category is the people that will use public transport very infrequently for varying reasons. It may be that they are travelling to locations easier to reach by train periodically, have to use it, not particularly out of choice, but due to a situation, or use it with friends to meet up and go out every now and again. They have the ability to negotiate timetables (just about) to get from A to B but can often find this stressful.

The third category is the people that never have, and never will use public transport because they just don't want to!

In an average year, I reckon I would use public transport around ten or so times, definitely putting me in category two.

Due to the broken leg incident however this year (which you will read about in a later chapter!), I have had to use trains and buses a few more times than normal due to my inability to drive and my urge to move around and get somewhere!

Just because I have used, and do use public transport on the odd occasion, I am definitely not the best person to understand routes and timetables. Let's just say you would never want me as a tour guide on the top of your double-decker as you'd probably end up at the wrong sightseeing destination!

Now you may be wondering why I am telling you about my lack of practice using public transport, but trust me, this is very relevant to my next story about my first date with my partner, Stacey. If anyone can turn a normal everyday experience into a drama it is most definitely ME!

Stacey is a Dog Agility Trainer. Think 'Crufts' with the arena and obstacles; tunnels, jumps, see-saws etc. If you are a seasoned watcher of 'Crufts' you would probably have seen her winning medals on your TV over the last few years.

I met her at a dog agility show she was running in the summer as I had some friends that happened to be participating. Now, these particular friends had a history of trying to set me up with new girlfriends to no avail, and 'surprise, surprise!' they were trying it again! I think on this occasion I will let them off however, as they managed to introduce me to my now wonderful partner, and mother of my child. Thanks guys!

After meeting Stacey at the dog show, we sent messages back and forth for several weeks until eventually we decided it was time to go on a proper date together.

Living about an hour apart we choose to meet at a Cocktail bar in Brighton which was equidistant between the two of us. As I am a gentleman (I would like to think so!) and this was a first date, I knew I would be coming straight home after the evening had finished, and as drinking and driving was clearly out of the question, the train it was!

I managed to get on the right train without a hitch and my navigation only went a bit awry when 'Google Maps' decided to have a hissy fit, and I couldn't seem to get from the station to the cocktail bar. After a quick phone call to ask her for directions, I eventually arrived at the right place only a few minutes late. Phew!

We had a lovely evening enjoying some interesting cocktails and getting to know each other, but as we know, all good things must come to an end.

We stood outside the bar, said our goodbyes and I started

venturing up the road towards the station with one thing on my mind. I kept telling myself, "No snog?", "Just a little peck". "What's that all about, thought she was keen?".

By the time I had got to the station, I had come to a conclusion that she was keen just evidently playing 'hard to get' which, between you and me, I sort of quite liked!

I went through my 'category two public transport user ritual' of trying to find the bloody ticket and double checked the info board to make sure I was getting on the right train.

The last train was at 23:42 and I was there with about ten minutes to spare so wandered over to the platform, boarded the train and waited for it to depart.

The evening I thought had been a success. I had met up with this lovely young lady, and pictured us sipping our cocktails together whilst enjoying the conversation, remembering how nice she looked in the outfit she was wearing and how bright the inside of the train carriage looked… Hang on a minute; something wasn't making sense… train carriage…

Several seconds later when I was a little less disorientated, I realised I had been dreaming the re-cap of the nights events and I had fallen asleep on the train!

When my eyes had finally adjusted back to being useable, my heart sank. All I could think to myself was "Shit, shit, shit!".

Straight in front of me was the information computer telling me, '00:45 This train terminates at Bedford'.

My panic was justified; firstly, I had no idea that trains ran straight from Brighton 130 miles north to Bedford, and secondly the train left at 23:42 and I'm darn sure that it doesn't take over an hour to get to Three Bridges, the station I was hoping to change trains at.

As the shock was setting in that I had fallen asleep on the train, missed my stop and was now stuck on a train north bound in the early hours of the morning continuing on to Bedford (ninety-five miles too far from where I live), one of the train guards came onto the tannoy informing us that a little teenage sod in one of the other carriages had improperly pulled the alarm chord. This meant that we would be stationary until the situation had been dealt with and would then continue on to the next station, London Blackfriars.

By looking at the trains and tubes on my phone, I realised I could walk over the Blackfriars Bridge once we arrived at the station, get on the tube to London Victoria and then get the train back to Horsham.

It was just my luck that by the time the train got into Blackfriars it was 1:40am and as I crossed the bridge, I was standing straight in front of a very closed tube station. Realising the last train out of London Victoria, going anywhere near my house was in seventeen minutes, I flagged down the next black cab and got him to drive double quick to the station.

I managed to make the train with five minutes to spare, and ironically it terminated at Three Bridges, the original station I needed to change at! Luckily a friend lodging with me at the time came and picked me up and eventually I walked through my front door at 3:45am!!

Now…. being the entertainer that I am, rather than shying away from my tale of woe, I decided to make light of the situation, by snapping numerous pics as I journeyed through London on my way home. When Stacey woke up the next morning, she was greeted by a story board outlining my little sightseeing tour through London!

Why she ever thought to herself; "I must have a keeper here!"; and wanted to continue to see me, I will never know?!

But now we are so happy living together, awaiting the special arrival of our little baby boy.

Maybe the Bedford train wasn't heading to the right destination but the 'Love train' knew exactly where it was going!!

6. APRES SKI

This story is a prime example of some of the typical 'Ali Antics' that 'seemed like a good idea at the time', but would definitely class me in the 'prat' category if ever there was one...

This was my second ever winter skiing holiday with my fun-loving group of friends.

After the first day of settling in at the Austrian resort, we had found our favourite watering hole and were looking forward to our first experience of a solo guitarist who played a regular set of acoustic covers at this venue. He was not bad at all! So much so, that by the end of the week he had managed to sell us a few of his CD's and kept us drinking in this bar for the duration of the holiday.

Having a few drinks in the evening with great music gets you chatting and meeting all the people around you. We started getting well acquainted with a few of the locals that were drinking in the same bar and as the evening drew on, dancing shoes were put on.

I don't know whether any of you reading this are a professional dancer, fancy yourself as a dancer, would like to be a dancer, or just throw in some moves on the dance floor as you see fit; and honestly, I don't know which category I would put myself in, but it is definitely not the first. Most people that know me and have seen what I'm capable of would probably put me in the latter!

On this particular night, what I like to refer to as 'The dancing circle' started to form. For those of you not familiar with this term, it is where prospective dancers and spectators gather round forming a shape resembling something that looks like a circle!

When this happens, it tends to encourage anyone that fancies a go at busting their dance moves in front of an audience, into the middle of the circle to display what they can do. It is a bit like the sort of mating display you would expect to see on a documentary narrated by David Attenborough!

My turn seemed as if it was fast approaching so just time for one more Jager!

I have always been a fan of break dancing, however the biggest problem is that I am not exactly the most agile or flexible person in the world! But tonight was the night I was going to give it a red hot go, and nothing was going to stop me trying something I thought I could probably do? Was it heck!

I entered the circle and threw my arms and legs out in various ways and at various angles just like I was in 'Saturday night fever'.

Then I took the jump literally!

Are you familiar with 'The worm'? If you are not, please bear with me as I try and explain it…

You start by jumping into a handstand but as your hands touch the floor, you immediately let the rear of your body fall to the floor starting from the chest and following with your legs. As soon as your feet come into contact with the floor, you push up again with your arms from the floor and let the momentum of your body follow itself back down again from head to toe. Imagine it looking a bit like the motion of a wave with your body, if it is done properly.

You would be correct if you were thinking that mine wasn't done properly!

I attempted the first part but jumped way too high and by the time I was heading to the floor in a handstand position, I realised "I'm not sure actually how you are supposed to do this."

By the time this thought had entered my mind, my hands

had come into contact with the floor and this was soon followed by my face!

Forces of gravity and speed were not on my side this night, and as I had jumped too steep in the air, my arms couldn't support the weight that was coming after them. The surface of the floor was made of hard ceramic tiles, and when my face made contact an instant pain shot through my mouth.

I am a seasoned performer, so I knew that everyone was watching, the cheering was continuing, and a performance was still needed. So, I continued. Well, continued as best as I could bearing in mind that I still did not know how to correctly perform the worm!

As I finished the not so great performance, I was met with cheers, backslapping and hugs from all nationalities present.

I felt great!

The next morning as I woke up with a sore mouth, looked in the mirror at my reflection, and saw a young man sporting a swollen cut lip, with bruising round the mouth, and missing half a front tooth, I felt not so great!

Even now this story still gets brought up in conversations with the friends that were on this holiday, and of course living with missing part of my front tooth will always be there.

But now, when I think something seems like a good idea at the time (there it is!) I always just slow down, drop down a gear, pause, and try and think about what I am about to do, what the consequences might be, and whether or not it is really worth doing at all.

Sustaining injuries from what my partner refers to as 'being a prat', in all honesty, really aren't worth it!

Lesson learned.

7. WHY NOT TO BE A TURTLE

This next story, you will be pleased to hear, didn't result in any particularly nasty or long-suffering injury, just another dent in my pride maybe!

I am going to hope I am not the only person that has done this, but have you ever been somewhere, in some situation where you have seen an opportunity to create a game?

Well in this instance I did just that. It was named 'The Table Turtle Challenge'.

It was winter last year and I was with a few friends enjoying a beverage in the local pub after work, and being cold outside, we were all seated around a table just in front of the fire.

At this point, let me describe the table as this is fundamentally important to this story. It was a two-tier table made from a hardwood (particular identity unknown at this stage), so as a piece of furniture it had quite a bit of weight to it.

The tabletop consisted of two folding leaf sections that opened in the middle to access the lower tier underneath. This lower part was supposed to be used as a magazine shelf or something similar, but at this stage was empty.

As we were gathered round this table enjoying the heat of the fire a friend points at the table and wonders whether or not someone would be able to crawl through the gap between the lower level and the tabletop. Of course, old muggins here says: "Yeah, I reckon so."

For me, this is pretty much the same as accepting a challenge that hasn't really been officially set yet.

Word quickly spread like wildfire round the pub and before long a crowd has gathered to see me try my best to crawl through this not so vast void.

Upon positioning myself at one end of the table and assessing how best to proceed, I made a comment that if I managed to crawl through the table and get my head out the far end, arms out the side, with my feet still poking out the bottom, from a birds-eye view you would appear to be a turtle with a table as a shell. Hence the birth of 'The Table Turtle Challenge'!

Like most things, the best-laid plans don't always work out as they are intended.

I entered the gap with my head tilted to one side, as it simply would not fit in being straight.

I squeezed my body in as far as I could and then realised my bum was having no chance of following my body and could not get through the table fitting in to the space.

My initial thought was to back up out of the table and hatch a plan B, approaching this from a different angle (quite literally!), however, upon further wriggling I realised I was stuck!

Sounds of laughter were reverberating round the room, and straight away one half of the centre leaf section had been lifted so everyone could see my very red face as I was laughing so hard!

None of us had noticed a metal rod running underneath the centre of the tabletop, which was now running along my lower back and had sandwiched me in the hole. After being pulled and pushed from every angle, I eventually wriggled back out the way I came in, somewhat out of breath and very much feeling like I had been defeated by a table.

Now I am not someone who gives up easily and when there is something in my head I have decided to do, then I will do my damnedest to try and achieve it!

I am not exactly sure where this brainwave came from at this point, but I thought that if I removed my builder style work trousers and the belt, it would make me more streamlined to glide through the gap in the table without getting stuck.

And so, the second attempt began...

Now just with my work t-shirt and boxer shorts on standing in my local pub, I manoeuvred myself into position. As you would have probably already guessed, removing my work trousers made no difference whatsoever, as this had still not altered the size of my bum, which was still the initial problem. And so it is not surprising that I got to exactly the same place as before!

Being called the 'Table Turtle Challenge', I was completely gutted that I had not managed to achieve this miraculous transition from Ali to Table Turtle!

Then came plan C...

I signalled to a couple of the guys to approach and lift the leaf section on the top of the table so I could talk to them. I relayed my plan, which was, with assistance I could stand up still inside the table as my body was already wedged inside, but my legs would be out the bottom, and I would be able to stick my arms out the side.

At least I would look like a hibernating tortoise, even if I couldn't quite make it to a complete Table Turtle!

With a lot of strength, my friends managed to lift the table with half of me inside it into a standing position, which I would like to say was met with a round of applause and much cheering from the spectators.

After doing a little dance and taking some pictures, the table was rested back into place and once again I went through the very hard work of removing myself from my temporary shell.

Now this all seemed like a great laugh at the time, but it wasn't until the following day at work that I noticed the movement of my back was very painful and quite restricted.

The weight of the hardwood table, combined with the metal rod that had been pushing down on the bottom of my back more and more as I was standing up and stupidly jumping around 'like a prat', had merely bruised the muscles on this occasion, so no serious damage, but it made the next few days' very hard work.

What did I learn from this little escapade?

I still live by the view of 'if at first you don't succeed, try, try, try again' but I think before I jump straight into something like this next time, I may evaluate the situation a little bit more.

Points to consider:

1. If it seems like an impossible task, it's probably best not to attempt it.

2. If the first attempt fails, will any further attempts cause injury that could be avoided?

3. Will anything actually be gained from achieving the said feat with the risks involved?

4. Are you just being a prat?

So, with hindsight being a wonderful thing, I will definitely be more cautious when inventing new games on the spur of the moment. Me being me, I know I will still have some great ideas, but will certainly be vetting any outrageous games in my head a bit more before any action occurs!

8. GOOD LUCK, BREAK A LEG!

When I was in Secondary School and then College, I developed a large network of friends but there were a handful of what I would call 'close friends' that I have always stayed in touch with.

We live in different parts of the UK and even different countries, but we will always find time at least once or twice a year if we can to meet up. I would say that we are all growing up now, but to be more realistic, let's just say we are all getting older!

Lover's turn into girlfriends, girlfriends turn into fiancées and then the weddings come around for fiancées to become wives.

On this occasion one of my good friends was about to wed a lovely Spanish lady in Madrid. The wedding date was set, invites were sent out and this would be my first experience of a Spanish style wedding.

The hotel we were staying in was a lovely four-star residence with a grand entrance lobby, top floor pool bar and terrace, huge lavish bedroom suites (when you got a free upgrade like we did!) and great friendly staff.

Most of the UK contingent stayed in this same hotel, and as we had a day or so before the wedding, we all enjoyed the time sunning ourselves in the Madrid sunshine and catching up from where we last left off.

As Saturday evening drew closer, we left the terrace, dispersed to our rooms to get ready for the wedding and gathered in the lobby to make the five-minute walk to the coach.

This was the first time Stacey and I have had a proper reason to dress up in our finery and go out together and I'll tell you what, even with her being twenty-three weeks pregnant, she looked gorgeous (I don't think I scrubbed up too bad myself either!).

The location we were travelling to was beautiful. We turned off the main road and continued down a windy dusty road for about a quarter of a mile till we pulled up in front of a quaint stereotypical looking Spanish villa with an archway and rows of chairs set out in the front garden ready for the ceremony.

Despite the ceremony being mainly in Spanish, we got the general gist and it certainly was a lovely moment. This was followed by drinks and tapas closer to the house, and later on a meal and speeches on the front terrace.

Boys being boys we couldn't forgo the opportunity to have a Cuban cigar and liqueurs to finish, and then everyone gravitated towards the courtyard area in the centre of the building ready for the first dance and disco time!

The montage of embarrassing photos of the bride and groom on the projector screen had been done, and now the dancing was in full swing. Now, being a Spanish wedding, everything was scheduled slightly later than you would anticipate in the UK, so it wasn't that long from the start of the disco till the first coach at 1am was ready to depart.

Being twenty-three weeks pregnant Stacey left on this coach, but as a good friend of the groom I felt it was my duty to wait for the 4am coach and return to the hotel later with the lads.

Another couple of hours go by and as the end of the celebration was looming, I had an idea.

Yes! Another idea that seemed like it was good at the time!!

There is no blame sharing here, it is purely a point that I would like to raise and for you to ponder.

On occasions, Stacey sometimes has to assume a more

'motherly' role for me, which just helps to keep me in check and most of the time stops me doing something really stupid... All I am saying is: if Stacey had not left on the earlier coach, and was still with me at the wedding, would this next incident have occurred at all?!

Having carried the Groom's Dad on my shoulders at the stag doo at a festival in the UK months earlier, some part of me decided it was a good time to have another go for old times' sake! I would have one more blast carrying him on the dance floor and one last boogie before the end of a great evening.

Now, I am not being judgemental here, but I would say it is a perfectly fair observation to mention that the Groom's Dad was a little bit bigger than me!

I crouched down in position, let him stand over me and had a couple of friends steadying him whilst I pushed myself up to standing. Things didn't quite go to plan though...

As I put all the effort into my legs to push up to standing, the weight accompanied by an uneven surface sent a very sudden shooting pain up my leg. This was because my ankle had rolled outward and had completely buckled as I was trying to lift him off the ground.

People instantly noticed something bad had happened and helped me over to some chairs where the initial diagnosis was just a sprain. This diagnosis was now being accompanied with swelling and severe pain, but luckily for me my friends were on hand to administer a sensible mix of medications in the form of whisky and paracetamol!

Do you remember that when I knocked my tooth out, there was an issue with the floor not being my friend? Well, I'm not prejudiced against floors, but we were falling out pretty quickly. The issue I had with this floor, was that as the building was of a Spanish style, rustic villa architecture, the courtyard, which was where the disco part was being held, was of a cobbled stone effect.

If you could imagine how uneven and unlevel this type of floor is then you would probably be able to see where this well thought out plan was seriously flawed.

Once I had managed to hobble to the coach, got a taxi from where the coach dropped us to the hotel (probably 200m!), hobbled through the hotel foyer to the lift, got to the seventh floor and down the corridor to the room, I wasn't particularly looking forward to telling Stacey what had just happened.

She was asleep, as by this time it was half five in the morning but of course the commotion of the two friends and I entering the room and moving towards the bed stirred her somewhat!

She did take the news better than I thought she would, and she got me all into bed and tucked up nicely.

After sleeping about four hours, the pain was keeping me awake and I when I looked down at my ankle and realised it had nearly doubled in size with some lovely purple bruising appearing around it, I thought it was probably worth taking a trip to the hospital.

The 'Hospital Clinico San Carlos' in Madrid, was a white building slap bang in the middle of the city and despite the massive language barrier trying to explain what had happened to consultants and physicians, the service was faultless.

I was sent straight to the A&E Department, had an x-ray, and they explained that I had broken the fibula in my right leg at the point it connects to the ankle joint. For those that would like to know it is known medically as a 'Weber B fracture'.

I was put into a temporary cast to fly home and out of there within a couple of hours. That was first class treatment!

Once home, I had various appointments where the cast was

removed and I waited to see if the bone would repair naturally. Unfortunately, that wasn't to be, so three-weeks after the accident I was back to hospital to have an operation with bone needing to be re-broken and plated.

As if sitting around for three-weeks already wasn't bad enough, the recovery time now turned into another eight to twelve weeks…

Maybe this was the turning point for me to really start THINKING BEFORE I ACT!

***

So, this leads me to the present moment…

As I write this book, I am sitting with my leg up, staying at Stacey's family home for the foreseeable future, with her Mum, Brother, Nan and Granddad.

I am here for three main reasons:

> 1. There is always someone at home if I should have a further accident, and with the nine dogs they have collectively, there is always something to keep me occupied (even just to watch) to save me from boredom.

> 2. Stacey can work from here full time for the time being. She normally works half the week from this venue and the other half from a venue near where we live. This way, as we are now on one wage, we save on unnecessary travelling expenses.

> 3. The hospital where the fracture clinic is looking after me, is only fifteen minutes' drive from here, so it's very practical.

I will tell you from my own experience that it is bloody awful to have to sit down and pretty much not move because you are glued to the couch through your own stupidity, all the while listening to the person you love and carrying your child, chatting with friends about you.

What you hear is: natter, natter, natter "Yep! He can't work for two months now, and he's self-employed, so not great!" and natter, natter, natter "No! he was just being a prat" and natter, natter, natter "I know, he is supposed to be the one looking after me!"

I hate the feeling of being a burden and pretty much useless, but I am being waited on hand and foot by the family, for which I will be eternally grateful.

***

Despite the downsides of having a leg in a cast and being rendered immobile there is one very important personal accomplishment that I want to share with you as a result of this injury.

I have given up smoking!

Now this is not meant to come across as a self-help quit smoking section, but if it does happen to help anyone for that reason then that's great! (The fee for that is included in the price of the book!).

I have been a smoker for the last twenty years, and although we all know that smoking is a very unhealthy habit, here is a bit of interesting information that I didn't know:

The nicotine you inhale whilst smoking can constrict the blood vessels in your bloodstream by up to 25%. This means decreased levels of nutrients are supplied to the bones, and when experiencing a broken bone, you obviously need as much nutrients getting there as possible to aid the repair and recovery; trust me!

It is actually suggested that if you are a smoker, then you can nearly double the recovery time for a broken bone, and in some cases the break will never heal as well as it should do.

Clearly this was no time to beat about the bush, and so I made the choice to go cold turkey and give up smoking.

I always said that I would try my hardest to be smoke free once my son was born, and after reading a self-help book; "How to be a first time Dad"; it does suggest trying to give up way before your new baby arrives, as the stress of giving up and trying to bring up your first child are not always the best combination!

So here I am, ten weeks smoke free, and determined to give it a good shot.

Even just this small amount of time hasn't been easy, but somewhere I read online that the best thing to do is to wake up each morning and say to myself: "I'm not going to smoke today".

It is so much easier just focusing on one day at a time, and not even thinking about the next day, weeks or months ahead. This way, you get a little personal self-congratulation as each day passes and feel like you are really accomplishing something!

It's definitely working for me!

9. WE NEVER STOP LEARNING

This chapter is really a reflection of some of the key realisations I have had whilst writing this book, and shares some of the insights that have helped me to move forward on my journey as I move closer towards becoming a father, and hopefully growing up to become a responsible adult!

I am going to start with a story about my granddad. A very special man, whom is no longer with us, but taught me many things in my life, most importantly that it is never too late to do anything…

When I was growing up at the family home, my Grandparents (Mum's side of the family) lived across the yard in a bungalow included on the property.

It was nice having them living so close, however as you have read already about my youthful behaviour, I was just as much a pain to my Grandparents as I was to my parents.

When my Gran died, my Granddad was the only Grandparent I had left (the Grandparents on my Dad's side having already passed away), and I choose to cherish every moment I had left with him, to benefit from the knowledge he had, and in some small way give back to him as much as possible as he aged.

After I moved out of home I would still try and pop up and see Granddad at least twice a week for a cup of tea and a catch up. He was remarkable; at ninety-six he was still getting himself into town to do his own shopping, tending the vegetable gardens, going for a daily walk, playing with his greatgrandchildren down on the floor, and many other activities that you might think would have surpassed him.

Sadly, at a ripe old age of ninety-seven, and after a long battle with a series of serious health ailments, he passed away at the end of 2018. The most wonderful thing I took out of his passing was that it was the first funeral ever I had been to where I didn't actually cry, and I am an emotional little soul!

In my own head, I feel the reason for this is because I had prepared mentally for his death long before his passing actually came. As I say that, no one can ever be fully prepared if you have that chance, as when it does happen it is still a massive emotional experience and shock none the less.

I was as ready as I could be, and mentally I had no regrets for one of the first times in my life of how I could have done anything differently. I felt I had learned as much as I could from him and had given as much in return.

I loved my Granddad very much and in the last ten years or so before he died, I was the closest I had ever been to him. Was it too late? Never.

This is a pearl of wisdom I will hold in my heart forever. He showed me that 'It is NEVER too late to do anything'.

This is a small excerpt from the eulogy that I wrote and read at the funeral:

"Granddad will always remind me of two of the last lines of Simon and Garfunkel's 'The Boxer'.

'In the clearing stands a boxer and a fighter by his trade,

I am leaving, I am leaving but the fighter still remains'

He was the best 'never going to happen, non-boxer' I have ever known and would even beat Rocky or Muhammad Ali the way he fought to the end.

Granddad, the fighter for me, will always remain."

To me a funeral should always be treated as a celebration of someone's life and filled with fond memories to take away of how you want to remember them.

In fact, I have regrettably been to quite a few funerals of family and friends in my lifetime and I stand by the concept of lightening the mood wherever possible. When I was travelling as I mentioned earlier in the book, I made the most of how inexpensive Thailand was by purchasing a tailormade salmon coloured suit in Bangkok. It is this attire, 'The Pink Suit' as everyone calls it, that is pretty much always the suit of choice for this occasion!

***

You are aware by this point that I am staying with Stacey and her family whilst undergoing my un-energetic recovery process with a broken leg.

It may seem ironic, but as I made the decision to start writing my own book, I have also had the opportunity to read another memoir that is very personal to Stacey and her family, and I have asked their permission to share this with you.

The book is called: "The Sudden Change In My Life"; and is written by Gary Irwin.

Gary is Stacey's Dad whom tragically died of a brain tumour in 1999 when she was only seven years old. The book is his own story about how his life suddenly changed after finding out he had a malignant brain tumour, and the serious emotional and physical journey that he then embarked on.

Meeting Stacey and learning about how she lost her Dad to a brain tumour, it seemed to echo my own journey with my head injury. As I read his word's I felt an immense amount of pride for this man that I have never known, reading about his own experiences in order that he could help others.

Gary writes: "I explain the treatments I have had and their adverse side effects; not only physical, but emotional changes as well. My reason for writing this book was to help families to understand how a patient feels and sometimes how a patient's personality will change completely. You must understand this is only my account."

This is such a perfect example of how people manage to deal with so many things, and still share their very personal experiences to help others.

Reading his words makes me so much more aware of the life that we have to live. The everyday opportunities that are available to us and how we can count every breath as a blessing. It showed me that not only is it great to talk, but sometimes it's just as great to listen. You never know what you can learn from listening to others and sharing in the experiences that they are offering.

Although I never met Gary, I feel grateful to have read his book, and learnt something from Stacey's Dad. Breaking my leg and living at Stacey's for two months, not only gave me the opportunity to share in his life, but to write my own memoir, following in his footsteps.

Gary Irwin, a credit to all and still very much loved by those special to him.

Learning is a funny thing, sometimes you learn something when you least expect it. Your awareness seems to shift, and a realisation drops in from no-where…

As I have been writing this book, I have had so many of these realisations, and I have noticed how many little changes I need to make in my life to really be the person I want to be.

However, it has also occurred to me that changing everything about oneself is definitely not the right path; for who would I be if I changed everything?!

Somewhere there must be a compromise. A way that I can still be myself, and simply adjust small details, but never getting pushed too far where I seem to have lost my original personality.

Let me use what I am about to cook for dinner this evening as an example:

Bolognese! When I cook it, it has mince, tomatoes, garlic, carrots, onion and varying herbs and spices. Let's assume that this is me as a person!

If I have no carrots or someone didn't like them, I could use a pepper instead. If it tasted better and worked with the pepper rather than the carrot, I might always cook it this way from now on. This is a compromise.

If I took out the tomatoes and pretty much removed the sauce, this is a big no-no. Suddenly it is not a Bolognese anymore and not me! This is way more than a compromise.

I have come to the realisation that, nobody is perfect (myself included)! Making little changes where you need to, will help to make you a better person. You have to find your own boundary where the compromises have reached their limits, but relish in the changes you have made for those close to you to enjoy.

I have put my parents through a lot in my lifetime, but I know that while they are still around, they will always be there for me when I need them.

Following the horrific car accident, I was in, and the phone call they received that night, I don't think that my behaviour from then and up to this point in time has been the most helpful.

When I phone them on occasions, and I start the conversation with "Hi Mum/Dad. Uh! I've had an accident..." I believe there will always be a flashback to that evening which I don't think they will ever forget.

I am about to take on a massive responsibility very soon with a little one on the way.

I have always wanted to have children when I was ready, but Woody was conceived quicker than Stacey and I expected and I now think I'm not sure there is ever really a time I would have been 'ready'!

The biggest stress I have about becoming a father is how I can be a responsible parent, when I can quite easily behave as an irresponsible child at times.

Well this final injury, and opportunity to write this book, ladies and gentlemen, was the final kick up the arse I needed to say "OK, now it's time to take the next step in my life to be who I actually want to be."

Who that is can't be explained or described to you in words. Those closest to me have told me that "growing up a bit", "being more responsible", and "stopping being such a prat", would be great, but to be careful not to change who I actually am.

The point at which I feel that is achieved will be something only I will know when it happens.

And when I do, I am sure my Mum, my Dad, my partner Stacey, and my son Woody will too.

10. AN EARLY ARRIVAL

As I said at the beginning of this book, my plan was to have it finished before our son was born, but alas I didn't quite make it....

Stacey's waters broke very early on a Saturday morning which happened to be five and a half weeks earlier than the due date!

We got all the bits packed up and headed straight off to the hospital knowing that a little 'Woody' was imminently about to arrive.

Whilst we waited at the hospital for something to happen (a very long 48hours of waiting), I had just enough time to add the last little bit to the book to make it complete, however my laptop had other ideas.

During these final additions, technology was not on my side, and I lost the final part of the book much to my frustration. Trying my hardest not to launch the laptop out of the second-floor window of the delivery suite, I put it all to one side, realising that whether Woody was here or not, it didn't matter when the book was finished.

What then happened for the next hour was one of the weirdest things I have ever experienced in my life. Stacey was induced and changes were happening, contractions were starting and things were getting real!

I can't say how anyone else was feeling, but I had feelings of joy, worry, excitement and most of all anticipation, all at the same time.

At 00:48 on 11/11/2019 and weighing in at 5lb 6oz (bigger than most people were expecting being five and a half weeks early), Woody entered this world fit and strong!

I didn't quite get the book finished before he arrived, but my biggest inspiration for having even done this at all, decided to show up and now I got to meet my son for the first time.

***

At this exact moment in time, it is 10pm and I am sitting in a chair next to Woody's cot on the 'Special Care Baby Unit' at the hospital, keeping him company while his Mum goes for a rest and looking forward to having my first go at feeding him before I need to head back home.

I could sit here for hours and watch the little wriggles he does, all the funny facial expressions he's got going on, and the little noises that he keeps making.

This is what life is all about!

Seeing this little bundle of joy snoozing away next to me reminds me how we all started off in this life. Stress free, carefree and completely innocent.

Make the most of what you have and always remember, you are whoever you want to be.

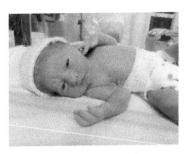

One hour old

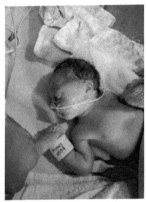

Three days old

Three hours old

Looking at each other for the first time that will last forever. x

ACKNOWLEDGEMENT

I would like to acknowledge everyone that has been mentioned in this book. Without these people, I would never have had the material to be able to write and publish my first book, something I never thought I would ever do!

A special mention however goes to my sister, Emily. She has spent a lot of her personal time being my editor for this book, and trust me, there was grammar, spelling and formatting that definitely needed doing!

Without her help, I'm not sure that you would have been able to read and understand what I have had published!

Big thanks to you Sis xxx

Lightning Source UK Ltd.
Milton Keynes UK
UKHW041539140620
364912UK00005B/1425